Ella's Umbrella

Written by Chris Powling

Illustrated by Sergio De Giorgi

OXFORD
UNIVERSITY PRESS

OXFORD
UNIVERSITY PRESS

Great Clarendon Street, Oxford, OX2 6DP, United Kingdom

Oxford University Press is a department of the University
of Oxford. It furthers the University's objective of excellence
in research, scholarship, and education by publishing
worldwide. Oxford is a registered trade mark of Oxford
University Press in the UK and in certain other countries

British Library Cataloguing in Publication Data
Data available

ISBN: 978-0-19-835659-2

10 9 8

Paper used in the production of this book is a natural, recyclable product
made from wood grown in sustainable forests. The manufacturing process
conforms to the environmental regulations of the country of origin.

Printed in China by Leo Paper Products Ltd.

Acknowledgements

Series Advisor: Nikki Gamble
Illustrated by Sergio De Giorgi
Designed by Kim Ferguson

Chapter 1

Grandpa

I love visiting Grandpa.

He's an inventor, you see. He's always making special things for me to play with.

Once he made a ball you can always catch, however high you throw it. He also made a pencil that can draw any picture you like!

"Soon my inventions will be in all the best toyshops, Ella," Grandpa told me. "Then I'll be rich and famous!"

I believed him, too. Or I did until last Saturday.

"An *umbrella*, Grandpa?" I asked, when I saw his new invention.

"It's not just *any* umbrella," said Grandpa.

I could see that. At one end, it had a propeller like a tiny windmill. At the other was a handle with lots of buttons on it.

"It's just started to rain," Grandpa winked. "You can try it out in the garden."

But when I went outside and opened up the umbrella, it whooshed me right off my feet.

"Hey, Grandpa!" I yelled over my shoulder. "This umbrella can fly!"

"Exactly, Ella!" Grandpa shouted from the back door. "So hold on tight and don't let go!"

Let go? That was the last thing I wanted to do. I was so excited!

7

Chapter 2
Test Drive

The umbrella took me out of the garden and suddenly I was floating just above the street. Luckily, it didn't go too high. The people coming towards me looked amazed.

"Watch out!" I called ahead. "I'm still learning how this thing works!"

My warnings didn't do any good. A postman
dropped his bag of letters. A delivery woman spilled
a tray of cakes.

"Excuse me – sorry!" I cried, as I swept along the
street, leaving all sorts of trouble behind me.

Just then, my phone started to ring.
It was Grandpa!

"How do you like the umbrella, Ella?"
Grandpa asked.

"It's wonderful!" I said. "But how do
I steer it?"

"Easy!" Grandpa chuckled. "Twist the
handle to the left if you want to go left.
Twist it to the right if you want to
go right. Just practise a bit."

So I practised a bit.

And guess what …

… it worked!

Soon, I could steer my umbrella anywhere.

I floated happily through the rain.

"Thanks, Grandpa," I whispered
to myself. "This is great!"

As I drifted along, I noticed a tourist in a big, floppy hat.
He was looking at a map of the city. I couldn't see his face,
but I felt sorry for him at once.

"It's not much fun being lost in weather like this," I thought.
"Unless you've got an umbrella like mine, of course!"

I thought the tourist seemed a bit
familiar, but when I looked
again, he'd gone.

Chapter 3
Umbrella Boat

"Where shall I go next?" I wondered. "Come on, Umbrella!"

It took off at once.

We skimmed downhill towards the river.

I meant to stop at the riverbank but got the timing all wrong. Instead, I fell straight into the water. My umbrella came tumbling in with me.

SPLASH!

My umbrella landed upside down in the water …

I landed the right way up.

I bobbed gently from side to side in my own
umbrella boat.

"Umbrella, you're amazing!" I exclaimed. "It's stopped
raining now and you're still keeping me dry!"

I grinned from ear to ear.

Just then, something on the riverbank caught my eye.
No, not something – some*one*. The tourist in the floppy hat
was back. He was staring harder than ever at his map.

"He must be really lost!" I thought. "Why doesn't he
go into a shop or ask a police officer? They'd be happy
to help him."

Chapter 4
Flying

I didn't have time to worry about the tourist. I'd spotted a couple of buttons on the umbrella's handle that I hadn't pressed yet.

"OK, Umbrella," I said. "Let's see what else you can do!"

But I must have done something wrong
because three things happened all at once:

my umbrella flipped the
right way up …

… the handle tucked
itself underneath me like
the seat of a swing …

... and the propeller began to spin ...

... and spin ...

... and SPIN!

I shot straight out of the water and across the riverbank, like a rocket on its way to the moon. Well ... maybe not quite as fast as that.

I gave the tourist a nasty surprise, too. My foot touched his shoulder as I shot past. It was an accident but it knocked him backwards into the rubbish bin behind him.

"Sorry!" I yelled, but all I heard was the sound of the rubbish bin lid clanging shut. After that, I could only hear one sound.

It was the zizz-zizz-zizz of the propeller on my umbrella

– yes, *my* umbrella –
Ella's umbrella.

I began to feel more and more proud of my umbrella. It was almost like a helicopter!

I soared **UP**

and **UP**

and **UP**.

Soon I was whizzing over every corner of the city.

I zoomed through patches of cloud and patches of blue sky.

I swooped over hundreds of rooftops.

I did a final loop-the-loop around

the famous clock tower

at the Town Hall.

I landed near Grandpa's workshop as
neatly as a bird on a branch.

Chapter 5
Giggles with Grandpa

Grandpa was wearing a thick, fluffy dressing gown.

"Trust me to fall into such a mucky rubbish bin," he grumbled. "It took me an hour of scrubbing to get rid of the stink."

"Hang on … you mean it was you all along, Grandpa?"
I gasped. "*You* were the tourist with the map and the
floppy hat?"

He nodded and pulled a face.

"But *why*, Grandpa?" I asked.

"I wanted to let you try out the umbrella on your own, Ella.
But I couldn't resist coming to watch. I wanted to see if my
latest invention was as clever as all the others. And it was!
I didn't expect to end up in the rubbish bin though!"

He began to laugh at himself. I started to laugh, too, as I pictured Grandpa's feet sticking out of the bin.

"Everyone should have an umbrella like mine!" I beamed.

"Maybe one day everyone will, Ella!" smiled Grandpa.

"When you're rich and famous, you mean?"

"Exactly!" he said.

So the next time you're in a good toyshop, look for a ball you can always catch and a pencil that can draw any picture you like. But don't stop there! If you look a little further, you may spot an umbrella with my name on it – Ella's Umbrella!